THE LIFE OF ERNEST HEMINGWAY

by Jean Kalmes

D1002500

Design and Pre-Press by IconixInk.com
Photos Courtesy of the John F. Kennedy Presidential Library and Museum
PCUSA5213 • Printed in China

CONTENTS

Chapter 1   Birth and Ancestry   **1**

Chapter 2   School Days and Youth   **5**

Chapter 3   Moving On   **11**

Chapter 4   Chicago and Hadley   **17**

Chapter 5   Europe in the Early Twenties   **19**

Chapter 6   Influences and Results   · **23**

Chapter 7   Changes and Letter writing   **27**

Chapter 8   Key West, Florida 1928   **33**

Chapter 9   More Changes, a Safari   **39**
               and Mixed Reviews

Chapter 10   Purchase of *Pilar* and   **43**
               Deep-sea Fishing

Chapter 11   Martha Gellhorn and the   **47**
               Spanish Civil War

Chapter 12   Mary Welch and WWII   **53**

Chapter 13   Travels and Awards   **61**

Chapter 14   Ketchum Idaho and Final Days   **67**

A Timeline of Hemingway's Books   **70**

Bibliography and Additional Reading   **71**

Personal Note by the Author   **72**

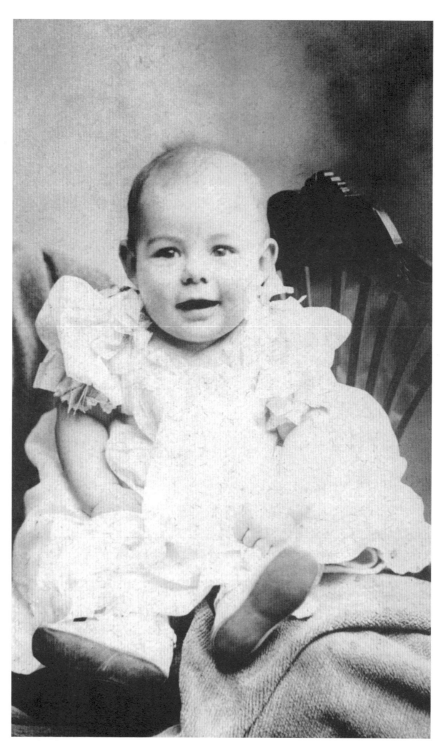

Baby Ernest 1899

CHAPTER 1

BIRTH AND ANCESTRY

Ernest Miller Hemingway was born July 21, 1899, in his mother's childhood home in Oak Park, Illinois, a suburb of Chicago. His father was Dr. Clarence Edmonds Hemingway, usually called Ed. His mother, Grace Hall Hemingway, had studied to be an operatic singer. However, when she sang at Madison Square Garden in New York the bright footlights hurt her eyes, and she decided that a performing career was not for her. She returned to Oak Park and married Dr. Ed on October 1, 1896. They resided in her widowed father's home and several children were born there. The first was Marcelline, who was eighteen months older than Ernest. After Ernest, followed Madelaine (Sunny), Ursula, Carol and Leicester. All were born at home delivered by Dr. Ed. Ernest had wanted a brother, but Leicester wasn't born until he was 16, so he never experienced the brotherly companionship he desired.

After Grace's father died, the family moved to a substantial new eight bedroom home at 600 North Kenilworth Avenue in Oak Park, which Grace had designed with a laboratory and waiting room on one end for the doctor, and a high-ceilinged conservatory on the other end where she gave music lessons. At times Ernest staged boxing matches in the music conservatory which had fifteen foot high ceilings and a balcony for observers. Boxing was a passion that started when Hemingway was young and continued throughout

Back: Ernest, Ed and Grace. Front: Madelaine (Sunny), Ursula, Marcelline

The new home at Oak Park, Illinois

his life. At first Grace earned more money than the doctor who was overworked and underpaid. Since she did not like to cook or clean, they hired maids, and the doctor shopped, supervised, or did much of the cooking and baking. He was also a strict disciplinarian of their children. He was sometimes nervous, and short-tempered, although he was very passive in regard to his wife who tended to be domineering. Both grandparents and parents were very religious and of the Congregational faith.

Dr. Ed was tall, dark, and handsome. He was often charming and had a wonderful smile, qualities which were passed on to Ernest along with his complex personality and emotional traits. From his mother Ernest inherited a defective left eye, artistic appreciation and an ear for tone and rhythm which influenced his writing. She also tended to be sentimental which sometimes could be detected in his writing .

Both of Ernest's grandfathers, Anson Hemingway, and Ernest Hall, had served in the American Civil War (1860–1865). From them Ernest inherited his interest in battle. He was named for his Grandfather Ernest Hall. However, he was not fond of his first name and often devised nicknames for family, friends, and animals. For himself he used numerous nicknames including Stein, Ernie, Hemmy, Hemingstein, Nesto, Ernesto, and Papa. The latter was invented before he was thirty, and he encouraged others to use it, signing his letters to family and friends with "Papa." The nickname illustrated his tendency toward sharing his knowledge in a teaching mode similar to his father's method, and his caring attitude toward friends and family.

Summers were spent in northern Michigan where the family had a cottage and eventually a forty acre farm. Dr. Ed was an accomplished outdoorsman and delighted in teaching both the boys and girls his knowledge and love of nature, hiking, hunting, fishing, and swimming. He took them on nature walks pointing out edible plants and teaching them how to survive in the wilderness. He had a rule that one must eat what he killed. Young Ernest enjoyed the months there. His experiences formed the background for some of his short stories, particularly the Nick Adams stories.

CHAPTER 2

SCHOOL DAYS AND YOUTH

A favorite pastime of Ernest's was reading. He spent many hours reading books from early youth and throughout his life. A lifetime friend from his early Michigan days was Bill Smith, who was also an avid reader and outdoorsman.

Hemingway eventually amassed an extensive library of thousands of books. It is said he once read the dictionary from front to back. One advantage of his reading of the classics helped him build an excellent vocabulary. His writing and love of storytelling was praised, encouraged, and appreciated at an early age although there was doubt sometimes as to what was real and what was fantasy.

Ernest attended grammar school and Oak Park and River Forest High School where he wrote for the school newspaper and magazine. He and Marcelline served as editors on the *Tabula* magazine staff, and both had a long list of activities they participated in from the orchestra and choir to the Rifle Club. He also sang in the Third Congregational Church Choir. Ernest was considered the best writer of the school's *Trapeze* weekly newspaper. He took boxing lessons and was active in sports. At age fifteen he grew to attain the height and build of his father, which was over six feet.

Since he was the favored older brother of a houseful of sisters, he enjoyed bossing and kidding them in a way that he used in dealing with women all his life. In his own life he yearned for a daughter,

Ernest fishing in Michigan 1904

Ernest at Graduation 1917

Ernest fishing as a teenager

and when that did not happen, he substituted women friends who called him Papa and he called them daughter. He tended to treat his wives somewhat the way he treated his sisters and expected them to hunt, fish, and enjoy the outdoors as he did.

After he graduated from high school in 1917, his parents urged him to go to college to study medicine, but he was not inclined to follow their suggestion. However, in later years he expressed regret that he did not have a college education. He complained that his mother insisted on a separate cottage in Michigan for herself and those funds could have been used for college expenses for her children. Hemingway achieved an equivalent of higher education because of his desire to read and learn through the years. His attitude, curiosity, enthusiasm, good memory, and his varied experiences resulted in a lifetime of continuing education.

Hemingway wanted to be a writer, but he did not have as a life goal a desire to be a newspaper journalist. However, his uncle, Tyler Hemingway, knew people with the *Kansas City Star*, an outstanding newspaper of that day. He secured an opportunity for Ernest to start as a cub reporter there. At first Ernest moved in with relatives, but he soon secured his own apartment and achieved a new freedom in a city much unlike Oak Park. Consequently, he began a new lifestyle that was far different from the pious ways of his parents and grandparents. He started to drink and smoke and spend time in bars. He was a hard working and successful reporter. He learned much about writing from the *Kansas City Star Stylebook*, which consisted of 110 rules for newspaper writing. He also learned all he could from other experienced reporters. Some of the stylebook directions included a positive approach, a concise, vigorous, yet smooth style, the use of simple sentences, action verbs, the best word in the best place, short paragraphs, and few but specific adjectives.

He explained that many of those rules served to shape the style he used in fiction in later year.

Ambulance driver in Europe in WWI

CHAPTER 3

MOVING ON

On April 6, 1917, the United States entered World War I by declaring war on Germany. Ernest had joined the Home Guard while he was a reporter in Kansas and enjoyed the drills and practice maneuvers. He wanted assignments that were where the action was, like bars, the jail, and the hospital. Although he enjoyed his job as a reporter, by the end of April of 1918 Ernest was ready to move on. His father discouraged him from trying to join the WWI effort. He cautioned that his defective eye would prevent his acceptance in the armed services. However, Ernest learned he could serve as an ambulance driver for the American Field Service Unit in Italy. He volunteered, received training, and was soon on his way to Europe as an honorary second lieutenant. He traveled from New York on a French ship, the *Chicago*, a name he thought was a good luck omen. He then spent some time in Paris and other cities in France before arriving in Milan, Italy, in June of 1918.

He soon found himself engulfed in a real war. In the first week he was evacuating the wounded by ambulance, and shocked to also be picking up pieces of dead persons. Before long he wanted to move even closer to the real action at the front lines and volunteered for more dangerous duties. One night he was riding a bicycle to take chocolate and cigarettes to the men in the trenches at the front. The Austrians hurled a canister filled with shrapnel which exploded

Hemingway in 1918

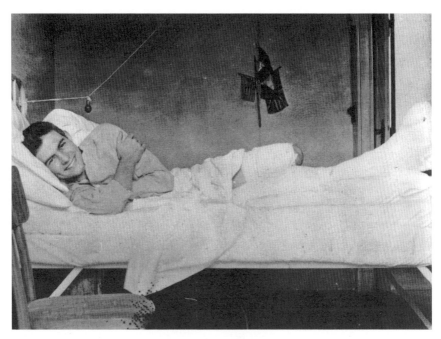

Ernest Hemingway in the Red Cross Hospital in Milan, Italy 1918

Ernest and nurse Agnes in Milan, Italy   Ernest continues to recuperate in America

and injured many. Ernest picked up a wounded man, and as he carried him, a machine gun sprayed his legs. At a medical station they successfully removed twenty eight of the hundreds of pieces of shrapnel imbedded in his left leg. He was then transported back to a Red Cross hospital in Milan where more metal was removed. He was hospitalized there for months. As a wounded American he was recommended for and received the Silver Italian Medal of Valor - He was later honored in the U.S.

While recuperating in the hospital, he fell in love with one of his nurses, Agnes Hannah von Kurowsky, who was several years older than Ernest. They talked of marriage, but she was hesitant to commit. When he returned to Oak Park, he wrote to her every day, but she eventually sent him a letter to tell him that she was in love with an Italian officer and planned to marry him. Hemingway was still healing from his wounds and the added heartbreak resulted in his falling into a depressed state. For a long time he didn't seek employment. He lounged around the Michigan property and his Oak Park home for months. He was difficult to live with, arguing with his parents because they treated him like a young boy, when he felt that he had earned the status of a man. After some time his parents asked him to leave, partly because he had changed from their pious way of life. He was drinking, and he refused to go to church. He did spend time writing. He patterned Catherine in his novel, *A Farewell to Arms*, on his memory of Agnes. He also shared his war experiences with individuals and groups. The news media and his own sometimes exaggerated accounts of what happened had given him the status of war hero.

He decided to move to Chicago where his friend Bill Smith lived. There he moved in with Bill's brother. Through friends he obtained a position writing for a newspaper in Canada, the *Toronto Star*. He also was attempting to publish his short stories in magazines because they paid well. He found it discouraging since he received numerous rejections, and his real desire was to get his work published and to establish himself as a serious writer.

Ernest Hemingway and Hadley Richardson marry in March 1921

CHAPTER 4

CHICAGO AND HADLEY

A t a party in Chicago in the fall of 1920 he met Elizabeth Hadley Richardson who had come to Chicago from St. Louis, Missouri. She was about eight years older than Hemingway. Nevertheless, it was a mutual attraction, and they spent many hours together until she returned home. Then he visited her in St. Louis. He was earning forty dollars a month editing *Cooperative Movement* magazine and writing news features. Hadley had a small trust fund of $3,000 annually from investments. They decided that they could live in Europe more cheaply than in the U.S. so they planned to go to Italy after their marriage. They were married March 9, 1921. While in Chicago Ernest had met a published author, Sherwood Anderson. He advised them that the place to live was Paris, France, rather than Italy, because there were many artists and writers there from a variety of countries. He also gave Hemingway letters of introduction to various helpful people: Miss Gertrude Stein, an American author with numerous contacts; Sylvia Beach, owner of Shakespeare and Co., a bookstore in Paris; Ezra Pound, a poet and writers' friend, and others. These contacts proved to be very helpful and influential for the young Hemingway. They rented a small, but cheap apartment and tried to live as frugally as possible so they had funds for traveling as well as the bare necessities of life. Hemingway also rented a hotel room where he could write in peace and quiet and applied himself studiously to serious writing. He also fought and gave boxing lessons while they were in Paris; therefore, balancing his sedentary hours with care for his physical fitness. His writing came first in the day, a practice he continued for most of his life. He also continued to write for the *Toronto Star*. The newlyweds managed to save money for hiking or skiing trips to Germany, Italy, Austria, and Switzerland. In 1923 they attended the Festival of San Fermin in Pamplona, Spain, a city close to the French border. This experience was their introduction to bullfighting, which proved to be the beginning of a long-lasting passion for Ernest. He was fascinated with the drama and suspense, the blood, the violence, and the danger. He was impressed with the men who used their skill, grace, and courage in the face of possible injury or death, and the bulls who were powerful and fierce. To be able to sit in safety and comfort to watch all this drama was like being a bystander at a war. Hemingway also developed a lifelong love for the country of Spain.

Hemingway was required to travel thousands of miles to various parts of Europe on assignment for news stories for the *Toronto Star*. For example, he was assigned reporting on the Graeco-Turkish War which was a dangerous site. Consequently, Hadley was often alone and worried about him, which upset her. In the winter of 1922-1923 she became pregnant which added to their financial and other worries.

CHAPTER 5

EUROPE AND EARLY TWENTIES

About that time another important and life-altering experience occurred. Ernest was traveling in Europe on assignments not only for the *Toronto Star* as their first European correspondent, but he was secretly submitting stories to other news services as he needed the money.

He asked Hadley to come to join him at Lausanne, Switzerland, in December 1922 for a skiing vacation in the Alps, and to meet new friends. He asked her to bring all of his manuscripts in a small suitcase so he could show his poems, short stories, and the beginning of a novel to a prominent American journalist, Mr. Lincoln Steffens, who had read some of his work. Steffens admired it, so he had offered to help him get it published. Hadley gave her luggage with the small suitcase to a porter and by the time she got to her compartment on the train the suitcase with all his writing had been stolen. She searched the whole train without success. Hemingway was naturally very upset at the loss of a year's work. Although he had attempted to get his stories published in various magazines without success, a few were saved because they had been mailed to magazines for publication. One story was *My Old Man*, based somewhat on Hemingway's father, which Steffens had sent to *Cosmopolitan* magazine for possible publication. It too was rejected and returned.

In later life Hemingway remarked that he had been working hard

Ernest and son John born in Toronto, Canada in July 1923

for a year to develop his unique style, but it may have been a good thing that his earliest work had disappeared. He was then forced to get back to work vigorously writing and further developing his own style. All his journalistic work was leaving very little time for his main purpose of writing fiction short stories and novels. The loss of his suitcase of writing, the rejection by publishers, and the exhaustion from all the travel and journalistic writing sent him into another period of depression. Drinking too many alcoholic beverages tended to increase the depression.

Also, at this time Hadley did not want their baby born in Europe, so they moved to Toronto, Canada in August 1923. To support them Hemingway was forced to continue his journalistic work by writing for the *Toronto Star Weekly*. He found the assignments frustrating and boring.

That year he was finally successful in getting some of his work published by small companies. *Three Stories and Ten Poems* was published in the summer of 1923, and *My Old Man* was published in *The Best Short Stories of 1923*. At first Hemingway had confessed to his friend, Gertrude Stein, that he was too young to be a father. Later the apartment was very noisy with the addition of a new baby, but he later wrote to others that they were a happy little family. John Nicanor Hadley Hemingway, nicknamed Bumby, a beautiful baby boy, was born in Toronto July 1, 1923. The Nicanor name was that of a famous bullfighter they admired. Son John or Jack (Bumby) eventually became the father of three daughters, Ernest's granddaughters. Two of them became famous as models and actresses, Mariel and Margaux Hemingway.

Ernest and Hadley were not fond of Toronto, and were happy to move back to Paris in January of 1924. Hemingway did visit his family before returning to Europe, but he was saddened as they did not approve of the type of stories he was writing.

Back in Paris they hired a nanny and rented a small apartment above a saw mill. Ernest again rented a hotel room and settled down to serious writing. In 1923 a small company in Paris published *in our time*. In 1925 it was enlarged and published in America as *In Our Time*, a collection of sketches and short stories. This finally brought Hemingway some of the recognition he had strived for.

In Paris he interacted with numerous writers, friends, and mentors, learning from them. Through the years he made many friends: some remained for years, others did not last a lifetime. This was partly a result of his highly competitive nature and his desire to be better than others at writing as well as almost everything he did.

CHAPTER 6

INFLUENCES AND RESULTS

Hemingway planned his time for writing the first part of the day, and then reading or other pursuits the rest of the day. He used this system for many years of his life. In 1917 he had definitely been influenced by the stylebook rules of the *Kansas City Star*, and he eagerly learned from more experienced writers. While in Paris he spent time at author and expatriate Gertrude Stein's home with its comfortable decor and many paintings by famous artists. She became his friend, his mentor, and his critic. Her home was also frequented by many aspiring authors and artists; Ernest interacted with them and learned from them.

Some of them were authors Ezra Pound, John Dos Passos, James Joyce, Archibald MacLeish, Scott Fitzgerald, and Sherwood Anderson to name a few. He met famous painters like Joan Miro and Picasso. He also spent time with another expatriate from America, Sylvia Beach, who was very kind and helpful to him. He was fortunate to meet others who frequented her bookstore which had a warm and comfortable decor furnished with many antique chairs and thousands of books. She helped him by getting *in our time* published in Europe. She was generous to him in many ways, including the fact that he could freely borrow books to read which he could not afford to buy.

Hiking and skiing in Alps, a favorite pastime

1st Wife Hadley Richardson

Ernest in Paris 1924

Hemingway spent many hours revising and polishing his work

Hemingway was developing what he called his *Iceberg Theory* of writing. He tended to write showing just the tip of the iceberg; that is, writing objectively, describing details of the scenes rather than stating emotions, letting the reader draw his own conclusions, and eliminating much of the obvious. He cut and revised numerous times to achieve the well trimmed effective sentences he is known for. He chose active verbs, well chosen nouns, and few but effective adjectives. He often employed conversation to move the action forward and capture the personality and motives of the characters.

He read and analyzed the work of famous authors which helped him in developing his own style. He admired *Huckleberry Finn* by Mark Twain in which Twain had captured and preserved the qualities and language of his day. Hemingway also used dialogue to move the story forward and create suspense. He used sentences of various types and lengths, often interspersed with participial phrases, revising often, depending upon what was appropriate to the action and the mood he was attempting to convey. Gertrude Stein stressed the importance of rhythm, which proved helpful to him. Thus, he learned to skillfully use word choices employing the repetition of vowels and consonants to achieve his smooth flowing rhythmic sentences and explicit word pictures. He tended to avoid the use of the ornate and flowery language of the previous generations, which were filled with numerous long descriptions loaded with adjectives and figurative language and stating the obvious. He worked by revising numerous times, cutting out the unnecessary.

Since his writing has been translated into many languages, and numerous writers have attempted to imitate his unique style, he is often credited with being the most influential writer of his century.

CHAPTER 7

CHANGES AND LETTER WRITING

Hemingway despised criticism of his work, and yet often criticized others spitefully. He was multi-talented, yet often felt unsure of himself, wanting to be the best at writing or anything else that he attempted. He was developing what in his opinion was the best way to write, while many other writers had their own style of writing which he considered inferior.

Although he was often generous and helpful to others, he carefully handled his own finances, and he decided against hiring either a publicity agent or a literary agent. This saved the ten percent handling fee. It also necessitated much communication by him. Many hours were spent and much was accomplished through writing letters. He also explained that he wrote letters because he enjoyed receiving letters. Letter writing served as a way of sounding off or venting. He wrote thousands of letters in different styles which varied depending on the recipient of the letter. His correspondents included his critics, his publishers, his banker, his lawyer, as well as his family and friends. He often apologized for writing hastily without correction as it was his way of unwinding and relaxing from the hard work of writing and revising. His talent for humor or sarcasm was more evident in his letter writing. He said he enjoyed receiving news and gossip. Sometimes he did not send the letters he wrote because of their harsh content when he was using them as a way of relieving his anger. Many were saved by using carbon copies.

Carlos Baker published a biography of Hemingway, entitled Ernest *Hemingway: A Life Story*, and he also researched, studied, selected, and published 600 of the thousands of letters Hemingway had written in his book, *Ernest Hemingway : Selected Letters, 1917 –1961*. Hemingway's fourth wife, Mary Welch Hemingway, also published some of her letters from him in her autobiographical book, *How It Was*, published in 1976.

It is interesting to note that the letters fall into several categories and subcategories. The letters to his family were usually pious and loving, while the letters to male friends were littered with profanities, criticisms, and blunt impressions. His letters to his publishers revealed his objection to criticism and to having changes made in his work, his need for advance funds for writing in progress, and his invitations to join him for various activities . The complexity of his personality is revealed much more clearly in his letters than in his other writing. He frequently sent letters to friends in which he planned travel or various gatherings where he would serve as the leader of the group. Sometimes these events were marred by his competitive spirit or his need to use boxing to vent his frustrations.

He generally shared his extensive knowledge in a helpful teaching mode about everything from fishing, hunting, writing, and traveling, to handing out fatherly advice. This aspect of his personality fits with his desire to be called "Papa,"which he used in signing some of his letters.

His concern for his first wife Hadley and their son John, called Bumby or Jack, is revealed in the loving letters which he continued to write to them all his life. He also had all the royalties set aside for their care from his very successful book entitled *Fiesta* when published in Europe in 1926, and the later American publication which was entitled *The Sun Also Rises*. It was the story of hard drinking Americans and other expatriates in Paris and Spain who had lost their former moral standards. His own morals had changed, but his upbringing came to the surface sometimes, filling him with sadness, guilt, and remorse.

In 1926 there appeared on the scene in Paris, Pauline Pfeiffer from St. Louis, Missouri. Pauline had served as an editor for *Vogue* magazine. She was a petite, slim, attractive, well-dressed young lady from a wealthy family. Since they both were from the St. Louis area, she became friends with Hadley, but soon set her eyes on Hemingway himself and made it obvious she wanted him for her husband. He became involved with her, and Hadley, humiliated, agreed to a divorce which was finalized January 27, 1927. This was a time when he experienced the feeling of guilt, remorse, and sadness at the failure of his marriage and the subsequent divorce, and the piety of his upbringing rose to the surface. But the appeal of wealth and the adoration of Pauline resulted in his leaving Hadley and Paris. Pauline was Catholic and he became what he considered a nominal Catholic so they could be married in a chapel in Italy on May 10, 1927. At first they stayed in Europe, but in 1928 they vacationed in Key West, Florida, were favorably impressed, and soon moved there. Pauline's wealthy uncle, Gus Pfeiffer, purchased a new car for them. The town was then an undeveloped fishing village populated mainly by the native settlers called *conchs*. At first they rented a home in Key West.

Hadley eventually returned to the U.S. In 1933 she married Mr. Paul Scott Mowrer, editor of the *Chicago Daily News*, at first in

Ernest and Pauline Pfeiffer were married in Italy on May 10, 1927

Europe, and later in Chicago. This proved to be a long and happy marriage. Because of their mutual interest in their son John, Hadley and Ernest maintained close contact throughout the years. He always wrote that he loved them. Also, friendships developed among the subsequent wives, Pauline and Mary, as well as Hadley.

Ernest Hemingway moved to Key West, Florida in 1928

CHAPTER 8

KEY WEST, FLORIDA 1928

Hemingway habitually rose early and applied himself to writing for five or six hours. If all was going well, he might continue; otherwise, he took off to go fishing or roamed around Key West. He enjoyed interacting with people and observing them for possible use in his writing. He soon developed a friendship with Josie Russell, a fishing buddy, who owned a pub called Sloppy Joe's on Duval Street. Other lifelong friends from Key West were Charles Thompson, George Brooks, and Captain "Bra" Saunders.

Hemingway was now famous and did not have to be as concerned about money and making ends meet, or finding a publisher for his work. Uncle Gus was generous toward them. This was a very productive time for his writing. He worked on *To Have and Have Not, For Whom the Bell Tolls, The Fifth Column*, a play, *Green Hills of Africa*, and short stories. He formed a partnership with Josie Russell in the bar. While in Paris there were few laws, and alcoholic beverages were readily available, but in the United States after WWI the Eighteenth Amendment to the Constitution resulted in the national prohibition of the manufacture and sale of alcoholic beverages. The law proved to be unenforceable and Prohibition was repealed in 1933 by the Twenty-first Amendment. Some states and counties retained full or partial prohibition. However, the use of tobacco and alcohol seemed common or almost a way of life for many in those times. Doctors, actors, and celebrities were seen in advertising, in plays and movies, using alcohol and tobacco. At that time the damaging effects of their use were not yet established. Key West was off the beaten track and little concern for prohibitive laws was in evidence during those years.

In 1928 Pauline was pregnant, and she wanted to have the baby near where her family lived, so they traveled to Piggott, Arkansas. Pauline had a very difficult delivery, and Patrick was delivered by Caesarian section January 28, 1929 in Kansas City. When she was pregnant again two years later, Gregory was born there in the same manner on November 12, 1931. Her doctor advised Pauline not to have more children which thwarted Hemingway's wish to have a daughter. Pauline proved to be a cooperative wife as well as an excellent critic of his writing. She devoted many hours to analyzing and editing his work.

The property at 907 Whitehead Street in Key West was purchased in 1931. Pauline also spent hours decorating and furnishing the home and planning the landscaping of the property. They hired people to help with the work, including those whose duty was to take care of the children . The house had been built in 1851 by a wealthy businessman. Coral from the site was used for the walls of the home which had tall windows to the floor, some of which could be used as doors to access the balconies of the home.

Bricks recovered from improved city streets were used to construct a high gated privacy fence for the property. The home was also unusual in that it had a basement, and eventually Pauline had the first swimming pool in Key West built . It cost more than the house and when Hemingway returned from a writing assignment, he was upset about the price. However, he enjoyed swimming in the pool. Pauline retained ownership of the property until her death in 1951. In 1962 Mrs. Bernice Dickson purchased the home, which was opened as a museum, with an admission fee of one dollar. In 1968 it was designated a Registered National Historic Landmark.

Ernest gradually discovered the joy of hunting and fishing in Idaho, Wyoming, and Montana. However, he was still passionate about the bullfighting in Spain which he attended for many years. They often spent the summers in Europe traveling to bullfights in Spain, collecting furnishings for their home, and interacting with friends. Since he could experience the blood and violence of war without the personal danger, Ernest thrived on the bullfighting . He had great admiration for the bullfighters, developing friendships with them.

Also, during those years Ernest acquired Charles Scribners and Sons of New York as his publisher and remained with them throughout his life. He produced much good writing in the years in Key West, and magazines now wanted to print his stories. The American version of *In Our Time* contained vignettes and sixteen short stories. He usually started with a short story and then developed some of them into novels. He believed fiction writers should write about what they actually knew. He had an unusual skill for observation and retention, and he based most of his own writing on his experiences, fictionalizing as he wrote. He was often asked about his philosophy of writing, but he was usually reluctant to be interviewed about it or to do public speaking about it.

Torrents of Spring, an unflattering parody concerning a former friend, Sherwood Anderson, had been published in 1926. In 1927 a book of short stories entitled *Men Without Women* was published.

The Hemingway Home purchased in 1931.
907 Whitehead Street became a museum.

Photo © by Werner J. Bertsch

It consisted mainly of action short stories involving men as the title indicated.

1928 proved to be a momentous year. Ernest's parents visited them in Key West and they met Pauline. All was harmonious. But then in December of 1928 Hemingway received the upsetting news that his father had committed suicide using his grandfather's pistol from the Civil War.

He was very depressed about this because of the loss of his father whom he loved. It was also contrary to his Catholic faith, and his attitude toward courage under stress. He now also became the financial head of his family. He blamed his mother as he believed she had driven his father to end his life. His father had financial worries, some from poor investments in Florida. His health problems, which included incurable heart disease and diabetes, were thought to have contributed to his death. Ernest arranged funds for his mother, wrote her a kind, yet commanding letter, and obtained a place for her to live.

In October of 1929 his novel *Farewell to Arms* about romance and war, with his themes of love and death, based partly on his own experience, was published. Over 100,000 copies sold rapidly in spite of the New York Stock Market Crash and the beginning of the Great Depression. This success definitely ensured his reputation as an outstanding writer, gave him more fame, more freedom to travel, and more freedom from worries about money.

CHAPTER 9

MORE CHANGES, A SAFARI, AND MIXED REVIEWS

I n 1932 *Death in the Afternoon* with detailed information about bullfighting interwoven in a fiction story was published. The critics had mixed opinions about its merits. Hemingway tended to overreact and did not take negative criticism lightly, especially in this instance when he was so passionate about the subject of bullfighting .

Many of his writings became the basis for plays, and for screen productions. This contributed to even more improved finances for him. He was usually unhappy about the results and the changing of the stories, but he generally just sold the rights to use the stories and did not participate in the actual production. The movie of his story *The Killers* was the only one he expressed complete approval of.

In these years Hemingway enjoyed meeting famous and wealthy actors, actresses, movie personnel, and other persons of wealth. With his own increased income and his interaction with them he discovered new interests, such as the challenge and enjoyment of deep-sea fishing and hunting in Africa.

In 1932 Pauline's wealthy uncle, Gus Pfeiffer, financed a safari in Africa with a gift of $25,000 for Pauline, Ernest and friends. Like Hadley, Pauline catered to Ernest's wishes. Since she hired caregivers for her sons, it allowed her freedom to remodel, furnish, and improve their home and grounds, to edit his work, and to travel, fish, and hunt with Ernest.

Ernest is showing his daring nature in a bullring in Spain

Ernest interacting with a bull. He is wearing a black sweater and white pants.

During the African safari of 1933-1934, Hemingway's growing competitive nature was definitely apparent. Many animals were shot and numerous mementoes were preserved and sent back to Key West. However, he spent a week during the safari in the hospital as he developed a serious case of dysentery and suffered a prolapse of the lower intestine.

During his life, he seemed vulnerable to illness and also seemed accident prone. His daring, his activities, and accidents resulted in many injuries through the years. Some of them were the shrapnel wounds, an anthrax infection, a scratched eyeball, a huge gash in his forehead, torn face, legs and arms, automobile and airplane crashes, a sliced finger, insomnia, frequent headaches, at least five concussions, a fracture of his right arm, sore throats, pneumonia, hemorrhoids, and kidney and liver problems. The latter were no doubt a result of his drinking. He suffered bouts of depression and thought being a man of action might serve to alleviate that. At any rate, he was famous for his writing and seemed determined to balance that with heroic exploits as a superior hunter, fisherman, and boxer. Just as his family's moral values and pious rules of life had changed drastically when he left home, and even more when he moved to Paris, now his father's idea of eating what was killed was changed to an attitude of seeing how many animals he could kill. He also wanted them to be bigger than the ones killed by others on the safari. Many wealthy people were traveling to Europe for the Grand Tour, and to Africa for safaris. Many mementoes of these trips were then shipped back to the U.S. From his experience, he wrote a book of short stories, *Winner Take Nothing*, which was published to mixed reviews in 1933. He wrote a nonfiction book about safari hunting entitled *Green Hills of Africa* which was published in 1935. It also received mixed reviews. However, two short stories set in Africa received outstanding acclaim ; they were *The Snows of Kilimanjaro*, and *The Short Happy Life of Frances Macomber*. Both of these stories were produced as movies.

Hemingway was as handsome as any actor, intelligent, talented, charismatic, forceful, captivating, energetic, and passionate. Women were attracted to him, and he also had a variety of men friends. In Florida he missed his literary friends as well as some of the outdoorsmen and other friends, so he frequently planned outings inviting them to visit him at Key West or to join him in places like Wyoming, Idaho, Cuba, Europe, and his favorite country there, Spain.

Ernest Hemingway fishing with Josie Russell

CHAPTER 10

PURCHASE OF PILAR AND DEEP-SEA FISHING

I
n 1934 he purchased his 38 foot cabin cruiser, *Pilar*, which was specially designed and built. It could sleep eight which enabled him to invite many of his friends to join him on fishing trips. He financed some of the cost by selling the fish they caught to pay for equipment, bait and petrol. He had been making fishing trips to Cuba with his friend Joe Russell and others. Owning *Pilar* made possible the planning of his own fishing trips to Cuba and other sites. It was a dream come true.

About this time, a young man named Arnold Samuelson who had grown up in a sod home in North Dakota, studied journalism at the University of Minnesota, and hitchhiked around the country, eventually arrived in Key West. He had a desire to meet Hemingway. He had little money, was arrested , and ended sleeping at the jail. Then he went to the Hemingway home, knocked on the door, which amazingly was opened by Ernest himself, and Arnold, tongue tied, not knowing what to say, just said he wanted to visit. He asked Hemingway if he would help him understand his method of writing and they talked briefly. Hemingway invited him to come back the next afternoon. He decided he needed a watchman to stay on his new boat *Pilar* in the harbor, and he offered to pay Samuelson to do that. So Arnold had a home on *Pilar*, and often interacted with the family and friends. He also helped with the fishing trips and took photographs, though he sometimes experienced seasickness when the ocean was rough. In times that were quiet and the fish didn't bite,

Pilar was purchased in 1934

Ernest Hemingway, Arnold Samuelson and Pauline

Hemingway discussed his philosophy and method of writing with Arnold who listened carefully and took notes on the instructions. He also had hours for writing when fishing trips were not planned. Arnold said that Hemingway acted toward him in a friendly and fatherly way.

Hemingway shared his ideas of writing: write about what you know, do not write too much at one time so you are exhausted, and stop while you still know what will come next. Then it is time to relax and sleep, and let your subconscious work. The next day, reread, cut, polish, rewrite, and then start to write again. When the piece of writing is longer, rewrite from the beginning about once a week. Hemingway stressed that fiction writing is really hard work, and he usually did not write with a fixed total plot in mind.

During the year Samuelson spent there Hemingway critiqued Arnold's writing and suggested ways to improve it. Most of Arnold's writing consisted of nonfiction articles intended for magazine publication. Hemingway advised him to just keep writing even if he received rejections. If his work was sent back by one publication, then send it to another.

Hemingway himself was still writing for magazines as they paid well. He obtained a contract with a new magazine, *Esquire*, and in 1935 he patterned a piece he wrote for them entitled *Monologue to the Maestro* based on Samuelson who played the violin. Hemingway was unusually helpful to Arnold, so it would seem the Samuelson - Hemingway interaction was unique . After a year Samuelson went back to Minneapolis, Minnesota. It wasn't until after his death that his daughter, Diane Darby, discovered his journals of 1934, and she and Eric Samuelson, her brother, in 1984 published the book by their father entitled *With Hemingway: A Year in Key West and Cuba* by Arnold Samuelson.

Ernest divorced Pauline and married Martha Gellhorn in 1940

CHAPTER 11

MARTHA GELLHORN AND THE SPANISH CIVIL WAR

I n 1937 Hemingway traveled to Europe to cover the Spanish Civil War for the North American Newspaper Alliance . He also published *To Have and Have Not*, the only novel he wrote that was set in the U.S. It dealt with the Great Depression and man's lonely struggle to be courageous and persevere in spite of problems. A movie was produced based on the book, starring Humphrey Bogart and Lauren Bacall famous actors.

Hemingway had met Martha Gellhorn, a fellow successful writer vacationing in 1936 in Key West with her mother, and was attracted to her. He renewed her acquaintance in Spain when they were both there reporting on the Spanish Civil War. His marriage to Pauline had begun to falter and they divorced in 1940, with Pauline and their two sons remaining in Key West. Martha located a property in Cuba which she rented because it was secluded for his writing and less accessible for fans and news people, and yet ideal for fishing. It was called Finca Vigia (Lookout Farm). Ernest continued his affair with Martha Gellhorn at various locations including Sun Valley, Idaho. He eventually married her at Cheyenne, Wyoming in November 21, 1940. She was quite different from his previous cooperative wives as she was an established author, and a courageous, competitive journalist. She accepted assignments in various parts of the world, often when there was a war or otherwise dangerous situation. Hemingway's three sons accepted her and she

Ernest Hemingway, always a
voracious reader, Cuba 1940's

Cojimar, Cuba

enjoyed their visits. Their wedding trip was her idea, which Ernest did not think was a very romantic journey, to cover the Sino-Japanese War in 1941. Martha did not like to miss a war.

Back in Cuba Ernest was working on his popular novel *For Whom the Bell Tolls* based on his experience during the Spanish Civil War. The main character was an ex-schoolteacher from Montana involved in the war and in love with a Spanish girl. In this book Hemingway revealed his altered opinion of wars and violence in general. He usually tended to avoid taking sides in politics, and did not think his writing should consist of preaching to the masses. Published in October 1940, his new novel was an instant best seller. A movie that was made very soon after, also proved to be a big success. Hemingway sold the rights to make the movie for over $100,000. The huge taxes he was paying, as high as 60 or 70 percent , were becoming a problem to him.

Martha tended to bluntly criticize him for his huge ego, his outright lying or exaggeration, his untidiness and sloppy dressing. He was drinking more, was unhappy, and his personality was changing. Martha was often absent on assignment, so he was lonely and he didn't like being alone, so their marriage was in trouble.

Hemingway spent time with his sons similar to what his father had done. He taught them to hunt, fish, and box. When they were apart, he wrote letters to them, continuing to give them fatherly advice.

Since he managed his own finances, much of his later writings was not published as he intended it as life insurance for his family after he was gone. He also wanted to avoid too much tax in one year. Some of the writings were not as concise and revised as he wanted them to be before publication and as he aged he found the revising more difficult.

Hemingway in the Biminis with a huge tuna

A favorite fishing site of the Hemingways in 1935 through 1937 was Biminis, located in the British West Indies, a series of islands about 45 miles east of Miami. According to his son Gregory in his book, *Papa, a Personal Memoir*, his father thought of the Gulf Stream as a river thirty miles wide. Its depth of 600 fathoms deep in places was where the largest tuna and marlin swam. Hemingway seemed obsessed with catching bigger and bigger fish, and in 1935 he won the competitive fishing contest at Bimini. The inhabitants were skeptical of foreigners and jealous of his winnings. He offered $200 to any man who could stay in the boxing ring with him for four rounds. He won all the fights, but was generous in giving the people fish that he and his friends had caught and in trying to promote the Biminis as a tourist destination. He had his family join him there and he rented nice accommodations for them on an island. He joined them on land, and they joined him for fishing on *Pilar*.

Hemingway often spent time writing and revising even when he was vacationing. In attempting to keep in good physical shape he used fishing, exercising, sparring, swimming, and playing tennis. Since he was multi-talented, possessed of a complex personality, and driven to be the best at whatever he did, this was not always conducive to his own happiness or maintaining friendships. He suffered with bouts of depression from time to time, especially after he had worked hard and completed a book, or experienced a life change.

Hemingway in Europe WWII

CHAPTER 12

MARY WELCH AND WWII

When World War II started, Hemingway was not eager to get involved at first. He wanted to stay in Cuba, and he did become involved with a project which consisted of intelligence work in regard to pro-Nazi factions in Cuba. Later, obtaining permission and equipping *Pilar* with special devices, he and a crew searched for German submarines in the Gulf Stream, but they did not actually encounter any. Then in March 1944 he was hired by *Colliers* magazine to write about the war, so he flew to London. Mary Welch was also there reporting on the war for *Time* magazine. Mary was vivacious, slim, petite, and pleasant, and he found himself attracted to her immediately. Both he and Mary were married to others; nevertheless, they became quickly involved. June through December of 1944, he was attached to General Patton's Third Army. He spent Christmas Day in Luxembourg. Someone arranged for Martha to join him, but it turned out to be a most unpleasant event.

Although his job was writing, at one point he became involved in actual fighting which was not acceptable for reporters according to the Geneva Convention. He was tried, but absolved. He spent most of the time with the Twenty-Second Regiment of the Fourth Army Infantry Division with his friend Colonel Charles "Buck" Lanham. He was involved in the Normandy Landing and the Lib-

Ernest Hemingway and Mary Welch were married in Havana, Cuba in March 1946

eration of Paris. He continued to write reports for publication alternating between the war zone and his hotel room in Paris. He also was involved in the Battle of the Bulge, where many died and the Germans were pushed back into their own territory.

After the war he returned to Cuba. For years he maintained his friendship with Lanham. In November 1946 Hemingway was in Sun Valley, Idaho when he wrote to Charles T. Lanham congratulating him on his promotion to general. On June 13, 1947 Hemingway was honored by receiving the Bronze Star for his contribution to WWII.

After his divorce from Martha and Mary's divorce from her husband, Mary and Ernest were married in Havana, Cuba in March 1946.

He purchased Finca Vigia near the little village of San Francisco de Paula on the hillside a few miles from Havana, Cuba, for $12,500. The estate had a swimming pool, a tennis court, and an acreage which was home to many birds, cats, chickens and dogs, including his companion Black Dog. There were numerous plants and trees, including fruit trees, flower gardens, a vegetable garden, a cow pasture, and a chicken coop. Mary did her best to be an ideal wife for Ernest. She put her own writing career on hold, adjusting her life to accommodate his needs and desires. She managed the household and the servants. She understood the necessity of his having private, undisturbed time for writing. She became a fantastic cook using the wild food from their hunting and fishing trips. She decorated the home so it was comfortable and inviting. She handled phone calls, news people, and other visitors who might disturb him while she skillfully accommodated and entertained the many guests that he invited. She joined in the swimming, tennis, and the hunting and fishing ex-

Finca Vigia (Lookout Farm) in Cuba was rented and later purchased

Mary proved to be an excellent decorator, cook and mate for Hemingway

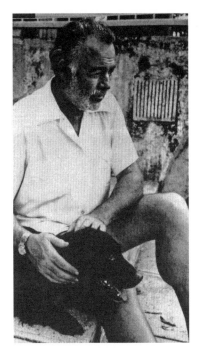

With his favorite dog, Black Dog   With his favorite cat, Boise

Ernest with another huge fish, a black marlin

peditions. She had a tall tower built near the one story house to provide a good view with a place to accommodate her sunbathing on the top story, one level where Ernest could write, a floor for their numerous cats, and a place for guests. However, most of the visitors stayed in a hotel in Havana. Some of the guests were the Scribners, father and son, and Maxwell Perkins who worked for Scribners and who was Hemingway's excellent editor for many years until his death. After that the Scribner father and son did the editing. He corresponded with them often and they became good friends. Hemingway's three sons accepted Mary as they had accepted Martha. Hemingway was very fond of cats and his friend, artist Pablo Picasso , had given him a special gift of a cat statue painted in his unique style. Ernest also enjoyed a painting by his friend, artist Joan Miro.

Hemingway started out to establish himself as an excellent writer with a unique style, and then to balance that, to show that he could be a man of action. He contributed much to the legend of himself, becoming a celebrity and a very newsworthy individual. However, this fame became a detriment to his private life. Although he was in Cuba, reporters, columnists, photographers, and fans constantly sought him out. He felt guilty about his divorces and his private life and thought it should be ignored, rather than publicized. Why not concentrate on the legacy of writing that he had worked so hard on that was impressive in quantity and unique in style that others admired and were trying to imitate in many parts of the world ? Why not forget about his private life ?

Although Mary devoted her life to being a good wife, Ernest's personality continued to change as a result of his health, his depression, and his life experiences. He loved her, but he was not always easy to live with.

He had discovered the American West and added fishing there, as well as hunting deer, game birds, bear and elk to his pursuits. They often stayed at a ranch where he could invite the three boys and friends, and where he could also write part of the time.

Later they found an isolated house near Ketchum, Idaho which fit their lifestyle. In August 1946 they were in Casper, Wyoming at a hospital. Mary was pregnant with what turned out to be a tubal pregnancy and she was in danger of dying when Ernest entered the operating room, took over to stop the bleeding , and saved her life. This was his last chance to have a daughter. He compensated by calling his young friends "daughter" and they called him" Papa," the nickname he enjoyed being called by many of his friends and his family through the years.

Mary, Ernest and Italian friend Adriana Gianfranco

Hemingway and Adriana in Cuba on a long visit in 1950

CHAPTER 13

TRAVELS AND AWARDS

Since Hemingway was a celebrity of the top rank like a movie star or politician, the press continued to cover his exploits, good or bad. He continued to travel, often with friends. They went to Europe, especially to Spain for the bull fights, and to France and Italy. He met an aspiring author, Franco Gianfranco, in 1949 in a bar in Venice, Italy. He became acquainted with his family and was soon very fond of Franco's nineteen year old sister, Adriana Gianfranco, another of his substitute daughters. Hemingway called them the *Venetian Branch* of the family. In 1950 Franco, Adriana, and their mother were invited to Cuba for a long visit. Afterward Hemingway wrote many letters to Adriana who was attractive, Catholic, and well chaperoned. She eventually married in Italy and the correspondence came to an end.

Mary realized that Ernest was attracted to beautiful women, and they in turn were attracted to the Hemingway magic ; she tried to handle this with patience. She also did her best to cope with his changing personality. Although Hadley, Pauline, and Mary had become friends through the years, they were saddened by the death of Pauline, who died unexpectedly in Los Angeles in 1951. Hemingway's mother, Grace, also died in 1951. At this time he made out his will leaving everything to Mary with written instructions on how to take care of his boys.

Ernest on the second African safari 1953-1954

In 1952 they were planning another safari to East Africa. They would visit Europe in the summer of 1953. In the fall of 1953 they would go to Africa, staying into 1954. *Look* magazine, a competitor to *Life*, which had profited by publishing some of his work, hired Ernest to do a story about the safari . They agreed to send a photographer along to Africa, promising a total of $25,000 if all parts of the contract were successfully fulfilled. Ernest's son, Patrick Hemingway, was then a warden and hunter involved with safaris in Africa.

One of the group included a friend from Cuba, who was an excellent shot. It happened that during the safari he was often out shooting Ernest. Hemingway was drinking so his shooting was not as accurate as in the past. He was also not successful in bagging the largest animals, which bothered him. He had changed and seemed less inclined to kill a tremendous number of animals, and instead seemed to enjoy watching them with Mary.

One day they hired a small plane to do some sightseeing in Uganda. In flight they encountered a huge flock of birds, which surrounded the plane. It resulted in a crash, injuring Mary with broken ribs and Ernest with a dislocated shoulder. Since the radio did not work, they were unable to communicate. They left the site of the accident, so when observers viewed the scene from the air there wasn't any activity, and therefore they assumed they were all dead. As a result they had the unusual opportunity of reading their own obituaries which were soon circulated by the media world-wide.

A second planned flight in a small plane a few days later also crashed and resulted in even more injuries. Hemingway had his fifth concussion, a fractured skull, damage to several internal organs, and some cracked spinal discs. The pilot had broken a win-

Hemingway with another huge fish

An early fishing trip with Pauline's Uncle Gus: smaller boat and smaller fish

dow and Mary and he had exited the plane. Ernest used his head to break open a jammed door for his escape before the plane exploded. He was hospitalized for a long time and his recovery was difficult and slow.

In 1956 his doctor put him on a strict diet to lower his blood pressure and high cholesterol level and to improve his liver and kidney functions. He also ordered that he drastically cut his use of certain foods and limited the alcoholic beverages. These measures resulted in much improved health. He started a number of writing projects which he did not finish and revise , but he finally completed and published *Across the River and Into the Trees*. It was a novel about a love affair between a young girl like Adriana, a beautiful Italian countess, and an aging army colonel. One critic said it was the worst book Hemingway ever wrote. Other critics applauded it, and it sold well.

Then *The Old Man and the Sea* was published in the popular *Life* magazine in 1952 with Hemingway's picture on the cover. It was praised by the critics, and the magazine swiftly sold millions of copies. The book also sold well and still is selling well after all these years. In fact, much of his writing continues to be popular in the U.S. and since it has been translated into many languages, it also continues to sell in countries around the world.

In 1953 he won the Pulitzer Prize for *The Old Man and the Sea*. In 1954 the American Academy of Arts and Letters gave him its Award of Merit. Then he received the treasured Nobel Prize for Literature in 1954 for his contribution to narration and literature. He decided against traveling to Stockholm, Sweden, to accept the award, stating his health was not good as he was still recovering from the plane accidents in Africa. The prize was accepted for him by American Ambassador to Sweden John Cabot, who read the speech Hemingway had written for the ceremony.

Hemingway's novella, *The Old Man and the Sea*, is a story of Santiago, an old fisherman who had been very unsuccessful, as he had not caught anything for eighty four days. He sometimes fished with a friend, a young boy. One day alone he rowed far out in the Gulf Stream and caught a huge marlin which he tied to his rowboat. Before he could get it safely home, sharks repeatedly attacked and ate most of the fish. Attempts were made to analyze the story, suggesting that the old fisherman in the story really represented Hemingway and his various problems, but Ernest stated bluntly that the story did not contain any symbolism. The old man was just an old man who could be defeated, but not destroyed, and the boy was just a boy, and the sea was just the sea, and the sharks were just sharks.

Hemingway was again the source of much acclaim, publicity, and admiration.

CHAPTER 14

KETCHUM IDAHO
AND FINAL DAYS

I n the fall of 1958 Ernest and Mary moved to a house in an isolated spot near Ketchum, Idaho, mainly because of the political unrest in Cuba where he had resided for about twenty years. The revolution and the ousting of the dictator Batista as head of the government eventually led to the rise of the communist leader Fidel Castro.

Ernest was in Idaho working on his autobiographical memoir of his Paris years, entitled *A Moveable Feast*.

A local teacher asked him to come to his class to discuss the art of writing. He disliked public speaking and was reluctant to accept, but using just a question and answer approach it turned out to be a very productive and enjoyable experience for all.

In 1959 they again returned to Spain for the bullfighting. Hemingway had secured a contract to do a story about it. The proposed 10,000 word story ballooned to 120,000 words and he was exceedingly frustrated as he was unable to edit and revise it as he had done in the past. He accepted some help in an effort to reduce the story.

In 1960 they again traveled to Europe and to Spain for the bullfights, but Ernest seemed to be experiencing a nervous breakdown. He had difficulty sleeping, was experiencing paranoia, and imagined the FBI was after him. The trouble he was having in attempting to revise and polish his writing was very upsetting. This contributed to the fact that he was often argumentative and difficult to live with. Though Mary tried to be patient and understanding, he sometimes ignored her or was verbally abusive to her.

In November when they returned to Ketchum, Mary persuaded him to go to the Mayo Clinic in Rochester, Minnesota.

He was checked in with other than the real reason and an attempt was made to keep everything very quiet. Hemingway was there a few weeks and received a series of electrical shock treatments and was dismissed. He was very distressed as the treatments had affected his memory and he was unable to write. He later went back a second time and had more treatments. He convinced the doctors that he was better and was then dismissed on June 26, 1961. Mary knew the truth and disagreed concerning the dismissal. However, they left and were driven back to Ketchum, Idaho by automobile, arriving on June 30, 1961.

July 2, 1961 he obtained a gun and ended his life in the home at Ketchum. At first Mary told the media it was an accident while he was cleaning the gun. It was a very difficult time for her. Within weeks, however, the real details of the story were printed.

A small funeral was held on July 25, 1961, where he is buried at Ketchum, Idaho.

In 1961 there was a United States ban on travel to Cuba, but President John F. Kennedy made arrangements for Mary to return there. Fidel Castro allowed her to select and assemble some of their belongings and ship them out of Cuba in exchange for donating the home and grounds of Finca Vigia to the Cuban Government for a museum. It is now an historical tourist site.

Mary Welch Hemingway established the Hemingway Foundation in 1970 and donated many photos, papers, and memorabilia to the John F. Kennedy Library at Boston University. Then in 1976 she published her interesting life story, *How It Was*.

Hemingway's great number of writings and the style he developed are his enduring legacy. He published seven novels, six volumes of short stories, a play, poems, and two nonfiction works. Many of his journalistic writings are also preserved. Since his death several of his writings that he had worked on, but which needed revising, have been edited and published.

Through the years many writers have created works of numerous types concerning Hemingway, his life, his writing, his family, and his friends. They include criticism, history, biography, photos, analysis, and miscellaneous articles. The home at Key West has brought many travelers since it opened in 1962 as the Ernest Hemingway Home and Museum. His name and fame continue on since his passing in 1961. His impressive quantity of writing and his development of his unique style using his iceberg method would be sufficient to gain him a permanent place in American Literature. All of his other achievements add to his life story. He was talented and bigger than life. He was a product of his time, his heredity, and his environment. If we consider the difficulty of his coping with fame, and with the demands of others, and how he was so demanding of himself in using his talents, we must also concede he was human and under much stress and pressure, possessed of human needs and desires. People seemingly remembered everything he did or said, and so many details, both good and bad, have been revealed to the public. This is a situation most people would find it difficult to endure. He remains an unusually memorable man of great accomplishments whose legacy continues to live on.

A TIMELINE OF HEMINGWAY'S BOOKS

1923 Three Stories and Ten Poems
1924 in our time
1925 In Our Time
1926 The Sun also Rises (Fiesta in Europe)
1926 The Torrents of Spring
1927 Men without Women
1929 A Farewell to Arms
1932 Death in the Afternoon
1933 Winner Take Nothing
1935 The Green Hills of Africa
1936 The Snows of Kilimanjaro
1936 The Short Happy Life of
       Frances Macomber
1937 To Have and Have Not
1938 The Fifth Column, a play
1938 The First Forty-Nine Stories
1940 For Whom the Bell Tolls
1950 Across the River and Into the Trees
1952 The Old Man and the Sea

Published after his death:

1962 The Wild Years (Toronto Star articles)
1964 A Moveable Feast
1967 Bylines (Journalism articles)
1972 Nick Adams Stories
1970 Kansas City Star articles
1970 Islands in the Stream
1979 Eighty Poems
1985 The Dangerous Summer
1981 Selected Letters
1986 The Garden of Eden
1987 The Complete Short Stories
       of Ernest Hemingway (hard cover)
1999 True at First Light
2003 The Complete Short Stories
       of Ernest Hemingway (soft cover)
2005 Under Kilimanjaro

BIBLIOGRAPHY

Baker, Carlos : Ernest Hemingway : a *Life Story*, New York: Scribner's , 1969

Baker, Carlos (ed.) : *Ernest Hemingway : Selected Letters* 1917-1961 , New York: Scribner's, Sons , 1981

Baker, Carlos (ed.) : *Hemingway and His Critics*, New York: Scribner's, 1961

Burgess, Anthony : *Ernest Hemingway and his World* , Britain: Thames and Hudson, 1978

Hawkins, Ruth A. : *Unbelievable Happiness and Final Sorrow, The Hemingway-Pfeiffer Marriage*, Fayetteville, Arkansas, University of Arkansas Press, 2012

Hemingway, Ernest : *The Old Man and the Sea*, New York: Simon and Schuster, 2003

Hemingway, Gregory, John, and Patrick (foreword) : *The Complete Short Stories of Ernest Hemingway*, New York, Simon and Schuster, 1987

Hemingway, Gregory H. Hemingway, M.D. : *Papa, A Personal Memoir*, Boston : Houghton Mifflin, 1976

Hemingway, Mary : *How It Was*, New York: Scribner's Sons, 1976

McDaniel, Melissa : *Ernest Hemingway*, Philadelphia : Chelsea House Publishers, 1997

McDowell, Nicholas : *Ernest Hemingway* : Life and Works, England : Wayland House Publishers, 1988

Samuelson, Arnold : *With Hemingway , A Year in Key West and Cuba*, New York : Holt, Rinehart and Winston, 1984

Note: I also read and studied most of his novels and many of his short stories.

PERSONAL NOTES
BY THE AUTHOR

If one is aware he will find Hemingway's name here, there, and everywhere all these many years after he lived. I have traveled to Key West many times and frequented Hemingway Home and Museum. I have been a literature and jounalism instructor at the high school and college level where I have taught his writing. I have read and studied much of his work and much that others have written about him. I have visited Ketchum, Idaho, where a bronzed sculpture of Hemingway designed by Robert Berks is located in Trail Creek Valley.

Presently I serve as executive director of the first Luxembourg museum in the United States located in Rollingstone, Minnesota, which was settled by a high percentage of immigrants from the Grand Duchy of Luxembourg in Europe. A Luxembourg friend of mine told me of a party in Luxembourg City during WWII when Hemingway entered and she said all attention became centered on him becuase he was so dynamic, energetic and charismatic.

It has been my purpose to write a brief biography for those who are curious, but not interested in reading a huge volume about him. I dedicate this book with love to my daughter Linda from Key West, who suggested this project to me.

Jean Kalmes